B

STUDENT BOOK

Amazing English!™

AN INTEGRATED ESL CURRICULUM

Addison-Wesley Publishing Company

ISBN 0-201-85367-1 Softbound
2 3 4 5 6 7 8 9 10-BAM-00 99 98 97 96 95

ISBN 0-201-49144-3 Hardbound
1 2 3 4 5 6 7 8 9 10-BAM-00 99 98 97 96

CONTENTS

Theme 1   New Friends   **3**

Hello, Friends (chant)   3

Hello, Amigos (excerpt)
Tricia Brown   4

My Day/Mi Día (excerpt)
Rebecca Emberley   8

My Best Friend (journal entry)   10

Hey, My Friend (song)
Bob Schneider   11

A Winter Soup Party:
Holistic Assessment Story   12

Hands-On Math: "Class Birthday Graph"   14

Theme 2   Family Times   **15**

Skidamarink (song)   15

My Aunt Came Back (folk song)   16

The Tree Boy (Haitian autobiography)
Nesly Bissainthe   18

Tangram Tales (photo essay)   21

Our Vacation (journal entry)   24

How the Stars Got in the Sky:
Holistic Assessment Story   26

Hands-On Social Studies:
"The Story Behind My Name"   28

Theme 3   Yes, I Can!   **29**

If You Can Walk (African proverb)   29

Terrific Tarah! (photo essay)   30

I Can (poem)
Mari Evans   33

The Knee-High Man (play based on
African-American folktale)   34

The Salt and Pepper Shake (song)
Bob Schneider   39

Little Ant Helps Out:
Holistic Assessment Story   40

Hands-On Science: "Jump and Count"   42

Theme 4   Busy Days   **43**

Busy, Busy, Busy (song)
Bob Schneider   43

"A" is for Astronaut/"A" es por astronauta
(photo essay)   44

Do You? Do You? Do You? (song)
Bob Schneider   47

Presents for America (biography)   48

Balloons for Sale:
Holistic Assessment Story   52

Hands-On Science:
"What Can Your Magnet Pull?"   54

Theme 5   Around the Pond   **55**

August (poem)   55

Why Rabbits Have Short Tails
(African-American folktale)   56

The Little Turtle (poem)
Vachel Lindsey   61

Busy Beavers (photo essay)   62

El Coquí (Puerto Rican lullaby)   65

The Little Lost Coquí:
Holistic Assessment Story   66

Hands-On Math:
"Make a Paper Butterfly"   68

Theme 6   Nature Walk   **69**

What Kind of Bush...? (Russian riddle)   69

Classes Under the Trees (poem)
Monica Gunning   70

The Ungrateful Tiger (play based on
Korean folktale)   72

Hands-On Science: "Sprouting Seeds"   77

Seasons, Seasons Everywhere:
Holistic Assessment Story   78

Index   80

New Friends

Hello, friends.
Hóla, amigos.
Allo, zanmi.

Welcome to school!

HELLO, AMIGOS

EXCERPTED FROM THE BOOK BY TRICIA BROWN
PHOTOGRAPHS BY FRAN ORTIZ

Hello, amigos!
My name is Frankie Valdez.

Art | Math | Music
Science | Social Studies
LANGUAGE ARTS

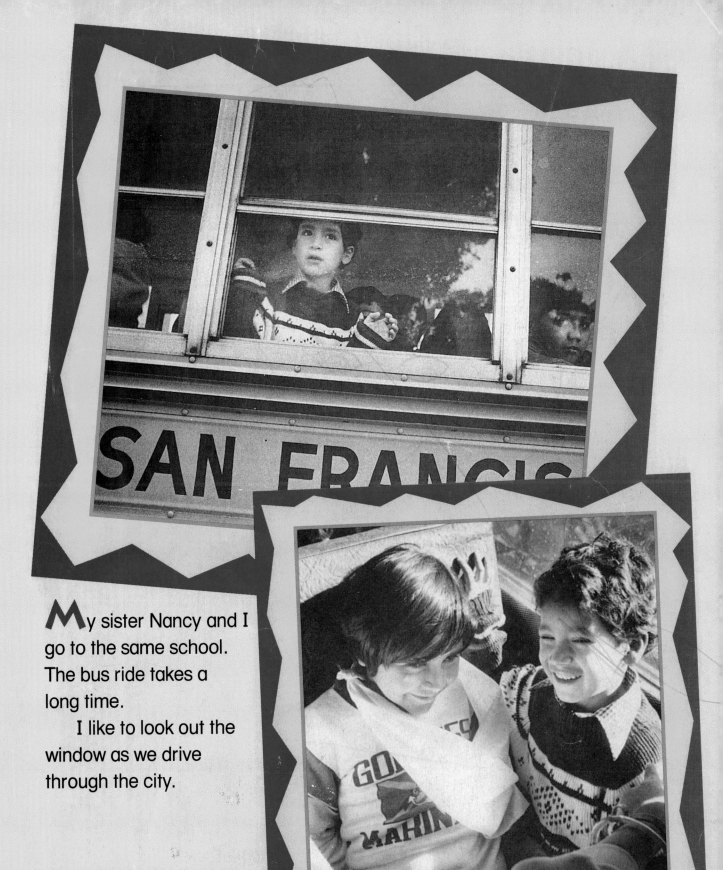

My sister Nancy and I go to the same school. The bus ride takes a long time.

I like to look out the window as we drive through the city.

I always sit with my best friend, Marvin Martinez.

At my school the first and second graders are in the same classroom.

Some of us speak Spanish at home, and we learn English here at school.

Our first lesson is math. Sometimes I don't get it.

6

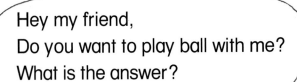

Hey, My Friend

Hey my friend,
Do you want to play ball with me?
What is the answer?

Say it again.

Yes, I do. Yes, I do.
Yes, I do. Yes, I do, with you.

Yes, I do. Yes, I do.
Yes, I do. Yes, I do, with you.

A Winter Soup Party

 LISTEN

 SPEAK

What has happened so far?

THINK

What food do you think the animals are bringing to Little Donkey?

Self   Holistic   Portfolio
Traditional   Performance
A S S E S S M E N T

 ## READ

Little Rabbit has a carrot.

"We can put this in our soup," he says.

Little Sheep has a cabbage.

"We can put this in our soup," she says.

Little Doe has some mushrooms.

"We can put these in our soup," she says.

Little Donkey says, "I have some potatoes.

We can put them in our soup, too!"

They all help. And they all eat the delicious soup.

THINK

Why was it cold?

 ## WRITE

Work with a partner and write a recipe for your own soup.

HANDS-ON MATH

1. When is your birthday?
2. How many other kids were born in the same month?
3. Make a Class Birthday Graph and find out.

Birthday Graph

January	Tuan Ahn
February	Shin
March	Jana Matthew Emily
April	
May	Tommy Javier
June	Marie Elena Mai
July	Julia
August	Nathalie
September	
October	Stefan Robert
November	
December	David

Art Math Music
Science Social Studies
LANGUAGE ARTS

Family Times

I love you in the morning,
And in the afternoon.
I love you in the evening,
Underneath the moon.

My Aunt Came Back

Leader: My aunt came back
Everyone: My aunt came back
Leader: From old Japan
Everyone: From old Japan
Leader: And brought with her
Everyone: And brought with her
Leader: A lovely fan.
Everyone: A lovely fan.

My aunt came back
From Mexico,
And brought with her
A fine yo-yo.

Art | Math | Music
Science | Social Studies
LANGUAGE ARTS

My aunt came back
From Guadeloupe,
And brought with her
A hoola hoop.

My aunt came back
From Niagara Falls,
And brought with her
Two soccer balls.

My aunt came back
From Timbuktu,
And brought with her
Some nuts to chew!

CRUNCH

CRUNCH

THE TREE BOY

BY NESLY BISSAINTHE

When I was small I lived in Haiti.
I did many things there that I liked a lot.
Right outside my house there was a
mango tree. I used to climb to the top
and eat mangoes with my friends.

Art Math Music
Science Social Studies
NGUAGE AR

Some people buy mangoes
in the market and bring the
mangoes back to their family.

It's fun for the whole family to eat mangoes together and tell stories. In my family, my grandparents would always tell stories.

20

TANGRAM TALES

My brother and I like to play tangrams with
our grandfather. Tangrams are a kind of puzzle.
Grandfather played tangrams in China.

Grandfather tells us stories to go with the pictures. Some of the stories are about the Fox Fairy. The Fox Fairy can turn into many different animals. He can turn into a huge whale, or a little rabbit.

Fox

Rabbit

Sometimes my brother and I make up our own tangram pictures. Then we ask my parents and my grandfather to guess what they are.

Whale

What do you think this is?

A ϯ

OUR VACATION

Last year, we went to Boston in our van. My father drove. My mother sat beside him. My sister and I sat in the back. My parents said "Don't fight." That was funny. My sister and I fought all week.

We bought tickets to the aquarium. We saw penguins and fish. But we missed the dolphin show. We all felt sad.

The next day, we drove north. We stopped
at a pretty beach. We ate lunch there. After
lunch, we got a wonderful surprise.

We saw lots and lots of dolphins. They were
swimming and jumping and diving in the ocean.
"We didn't miss the dolphin show after all," said
my mom. We all felt glad.

How the Stars Got in the Sky

 LISTEN

 SPEAK

What has happened so far?

 THINK

What will happen to the circle of light?

Self | Holistic | Portfolio
Traditional | Performance
A S S E S S M E N T

READ

The circle of light hits the mountain.
It breaks into thousands of tiny pieces!
The pieces fly up into the sky.
Anansi looks up.
The sky is full of little white lights!
"How wonderful!" says Anansi.
That is how the stars got in the sky.

 THINK

Why didn't Anansi want to take the light home?

WRITE

Make up a new story. Tell how birds or butterflies or fireflies came to be.

HANDS-ON SOCIAL STUDIES

What's the story behind your first name?
Talk to your family. Find out the story.

1. Who gave you your name?
2. Why did they choose
   that name?
3. Write down the story
   and make a name poster.

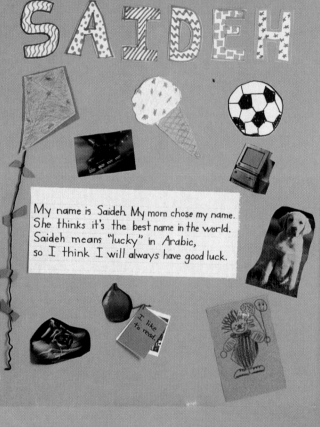

My name is Saideh. My mom chose my name.
She thinks it's the best name in the world.
Saideh means "lucky" in Arabic,
so I think I will always have good luck.

Art Math Music
Science Social Studies
LANGUAGE ARTS

Theme 2

Yes, I Can!

If you can walk
you can dance.

If you can talk
you can sing.

A saying from Africa

29

Terrific Tarah!

Tarah and her *Sesame Street* buddy, Prairie Dawn.

Tarah Lynne Schaeffer is nine years old. She lives in Connecticut. She works in New York City! Tarah is an actor on *Sesame Street*.

Art | Math | Music
Science | Social Studies
LANGUAGE ARTS

Tarah waits backstage for her scenes in the show.

Tarah has a disease called O. I. Her bones break easily, and she is much shorter than most kids her age. But Tarah lives a busy life.

She really enjoys wheelchair sports.

"I like going to the meets," says Tarah. "It's fun, and I make lots of friends."

Tarah is in the lead as she races down the track.

Tarah and Luis *(Emilio Delgado)* dance together.

We asked Tarah, "Do you have something special to say to kids reading this article?"

"Yes," she said. "If you really want to do something— even if you don't think you can— just try! You have to believe in yourself."

"Believe in yourself!"

I Can

I can
be anything
I can
do anything
I can
think
anything
big
or tall
OR
high or low
W I D E
or narrow
fast or slow
because I
CAN
and
I
WANT
TO!

Mari Evans

Art Math Music
Science Social Studies
Language Arts

THE KNEE-HIGH MAN

AN AFRICAN-AMERICAN FOLKTALE

Characters:

Storyteller **Knee-High Man** **Horse** **Bull** **Owl**

Storyteller

Once there was a man no taller than a person's knee.
People called him the Knee-High Man.

Knee-High Man

I hate being so short. I want to get bigger.
Horse is the biggest animal I know.
Maybe Horse can tell me how to get big.

Art   Math   Music
Science   Social Studies
Language Arts

Knee-High Man

Horse, how can I get big like you?

Horse

Well, eat a lot of corn. Then run and run as long as you can. Soon you'll be as big as me!

Storyteller

The Knee-High Man ate a lot of corn. Then he ran and ran until his legs hurt. But he didn't get any bigger.

Knee-High Man

Horse was wrong. I did just what he said, and I'm not any bigger. Bull is big. I'll go talk to him.

Knee-High Man

Bull, how can I get big like you?

Bull

Eat a lot of grass. Then bellow and bellow as loud as you can. Soon you'll be as big as me!

Storyteller

The Knee-High Man ate a lot of grass. He bellowed and bellowed until his throat hurt. But he didn't get any bigger.

Knee-High Man

Bull was wrong. I did just what he said, and I'm not any bigger. Owl isn't big, but he is wise. Maybe he can tell me how to get big. I'll go talk to him.

Knee-High Man: Owl, how do I get to be as big as Horse and Bull?

Owl: Why do you want to be big?

Knee-High Man: I want to be big so that when I get into a fight, I will always win.

Owl: Have you ever been in a fight?

Knee-High Man: Well, no.

Yes, I Can!

37

Owl
Then you don't need to be big.

Knee-High Man
Yes I do! I need to be big so...so I can see far into the distance.

Owl
Climb to the top of a tall tree. Then you can see far into the distance.

Knee-High Man
Oh. I didn't think of that.

Owl
Knee-High Man, you haven't done any thinking at all. You don't need to be as big as Horse or Bull. You're fine, just the way you are!

Storyteller
So the Knee-High Man stopped worrying about being big. He was happy being just who he was.

THE SALT AND PEPPER SHAKE

1.

and

and

Put your

On your

2.
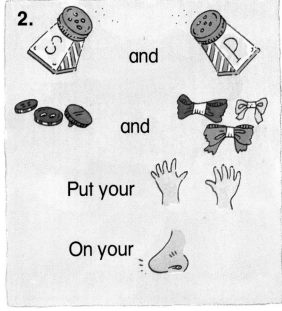
and

and

Put your

On your

3.
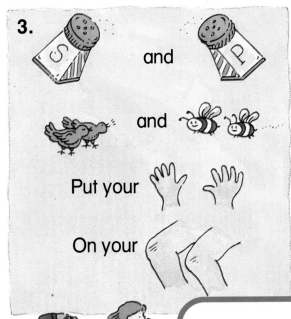
and

and

Put your

On your

4.

and

and

Put your

On your

Shake, shake, shake!
Shake all around.
Shake your body up and down!

Art | Math | Music
Science | Social Studies
Language Arts

Little Ant Helps Out

 LISTEN

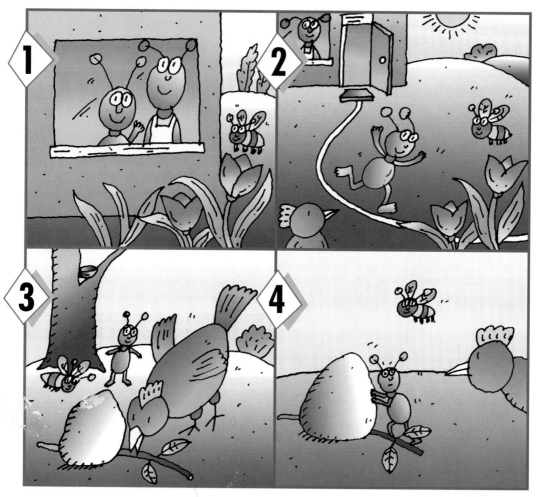

 SPEAK
What has happened so far?

 THINK
What do you think Little Ant will do next?

Self | Holistic | Portfolio
Traditional | Performance
A S S E S S M E N T

Theme 3

▶ READ

Little Ant called to her friend Little Bee.
"Please help me move the stone," said Little Ant.
"OK," said Little Bee.
Little Ant and Little Bee pushed and pushed. The stone finally rolled off the stick.

"Mother Bluebird," said Little Ant, "you can pick up the stick now."
Mother Bluebird picked up the stick.
"Thank you," she said to Little Ant and Little Bee. "You are good friends."

▶ THINK

Why did Mother Bluebird want the stick?

▶ WRITE

Imagine that Little Ant and Little Bee pushed and pushed the stone, but it was too heavy. It did not move. What could they do next? Write a new ending for the story.

Breaths in 1 minute

	Before jumping	After jumping
Deena	15	
Ben	17	

1. Count your breaths for one minute.
2. Jump 20 times. Count your breaths again.
3. What did you find out?

Busy Days

Busy, busy, busy all the time.
Makes me feel dizzy
When I'm busy all the time.

"A" is for astronaut
"A" es por astronauta

Near Lorena Street School there is a long, concrete wall. Once, the wall was dirty and ugly. Now it is beautiful. Children, teachers, and parents all worked together to paint a wonderful mural.

Lorena Street Elementary School, Los Angeles, California

Art   Math   Music
Science   Social Studies
LANGUAGE ARTS

Theme 4

Mrs. Harder, a kindergarten teacher, started the mural. She drew a row of children dressed in the clothes of different occupations. She drew a person for each letter of the alphabet. All the children wanted to help paint big pictures on the wall.

"When you see you can be anything you want, like a doctor or a dentist, you feel good about yourself."
— David

doctor
doctora

Most of the families in East Los Angeles speak Spanish. So the words on the mural are in both English and in Spanish. But there is room for other languages, too.

"Maybe new families will move to the neighborhood," says Mrs. Harder. "If they speak other languages, they can add their words, too."

Everybody is proud of the mural. Mrs. Harder says, "I always tell my students, "You can do anything. You can be anything.""

ecologist
ecologista

"People think about the hard work we all did, and they are proud. It changed the neighborhood."
-Gustavo

Presents for America

Long ago, a man named John Chapman lived in the state of Massachusetts. He loved the outdoors.

One day, he was walking in the woods. He stopped to rest and to eat an apple. Afterwards, he looked at the apple seeds in his hands.

"I'm going to plant these seeds," he said to himself. "I'm going to plant many, many seeds all over America. Our land will soon be filled with apple trees." And that is just what he did.

He started a long journey. He carried a bag of apple seeds on his back. He walked north. He walked south. He walked east. He walked west.

He planted apple seeds everywhere he went.

John Chapman gave apple seeds to everyone
he met. Soon, everyone called him Johnny Appleseed.

Today, we can still see some of the trees that Johnny
Appleseed planted. They are large, old trees filled with apples.
They are the presents he gave to his country.

Balloons for Sale

● ● ● ● ● ● ● ● ● ● ● ● ●

▶ **LISTEN**

▶ **SPEAK**

What has happened so far?

▶ **THINK**

What do you think Pig will say?

Self | Holistic | Portfolio
Traditional | Performance
A S S E S S M E N T

READ

"Oh, my," says Pig. "I don't want to buy a
broken balloon."
"Here is your penny back," says Goat sadly.
"Oh, no," says Pig. "You can keep my penny.
Please give me the yellow balloon!"

Goat gives Pig the yellow balloon.
Pig puts her umbrella down.
She dances away with the beautiful yellow balloon.
"Thank you, Goat," she says.
"You're welcome," says Goat.

THINK

How many pennies does Goat have?

WRITE

What else can make a balloon pop? Draw or write
some ideas.

A magnet can pull many things.
Feel the pull of a magnet.
What can your magnet pull?

Try these things.	YES	NO
a penny		
paper clips		
scissors		
pencils		
a dime		
a string		
a crayon		
paper		
a jar lid		

Art | Math | Music
Science | Social Studies
LANGUAGE ARTS

Around the Pond

In August when the days are hot,
I like to find a shady spot,
And hardly move a bit—
And sit—
And sit—
And sit—
And sit!

Why Rabbits Have Short Tails

AN AFRICAN-AMERICAN FOLKTALE

Once upon a time, rabbits had short ears and fine long tails.

Now, rabbits have long ears and short fluffy tails.

This is how it happened.

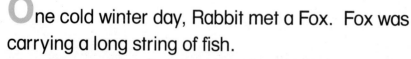

One cold winter day, Rabbit met a Fox. Fox was carrying a long string of fish.

"Where did you get those fish?" asked Rabbit.

"From the pond," said Fox.

"But it's winter," said Rabbit. "The pond is covered with ice."

"Yes, but I know a trick," said Fox. "Come with me and I'll show you."

Rabbit followed Fox down to the pond. Fox showed Rabbit a hole in the ice.

Fox said, "Sit here on the ice. Let your fine long tail hang down into the water. Stay here all night. In the morning you'll have a string of fish on your tail."

So Rabbit sat on the ice. He let his fine long tail hang down into the water. He sat and sat and sat all night. It was very cold and very uncomfortable, but Rabbit kept thinking of the wonderful fried fish he would have for breakfast.

Finally, morning came. "It's time to pull up my fish!" said Rabbit. Rabbit tried to stand up, but his tail was frozen in the ice! "Help, help! I'm stuck!" cried Rabbit.

Owl heard Rabbit. She came to help. "I will pull you by your ears," said Owl. "Then you will not be stuck."

Owl pulled Rabbit by his ears. She pulled and pulled. Rabbit's ears got longer and longer, but he was still stuck in the ice.

"I think we need more help," said Owl.

All Rabbit's friends came down to the pond to help. They pulled and pulled and pulled. Finally, Rabbit was free, but his fine long tail stayed in the ice. All that remained was a short fluffy cotton tail.

That is why today all rabbits have long ears and short tails. And whenever they see a fox, they run the other way!

THE LITTLE TURTLE

There was a little turtle.
He lived in a box.
He swam in a puddle.
He climbed the rocks.

He snapped at a mosquito.
He snapped at a flea.
He snapped at a minnow.
And he snapped at me.

He caught the mosquito.
He caught the flea.
He caught the minnow.
But he didn't catch me.

Vachel Lindsey

Art | Math | Music
Science | Social Studies
LANGUAGE AR

Busy Beavers

Beavers build their homes from trees. They chew down the trees with their big front teeth.

A beaver's home is called a lodge. Beavers build their lodges in the middle of ponds.

The lodges have mud floors. The beavers eat and sleep on the mud floor.

Art | Math | Music
Science | Social Studies

LANGUAGE ARTS

Beavers eat leaves and tree bark. They store tree branches at the bottom of the pond. These branches are food for the winter.

When the top of the pond freezes over, beavers bring the branches into their lodge. If all the pond freezes, beavers still have food. They eat the walls of their lodge!

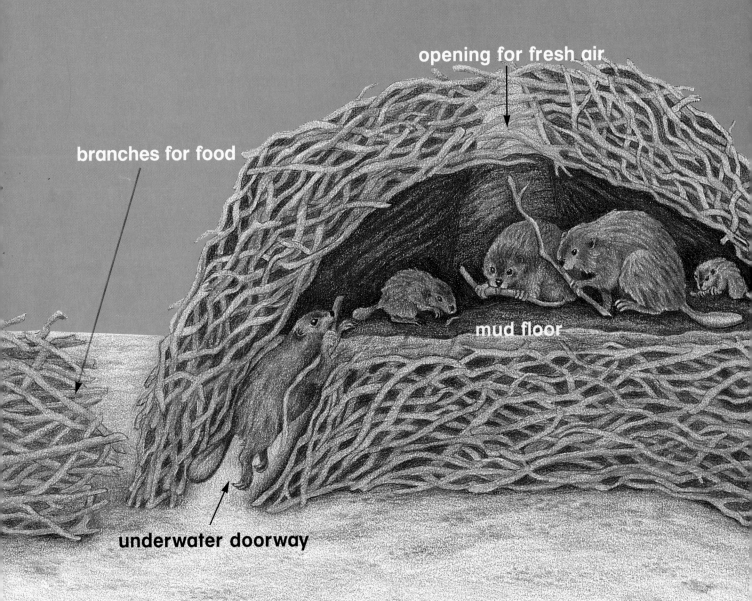

opening for fresh air

branches for food

mud floor

underwater doorway

Beavers are good swimmers. Baby beavers learn
how to swim when they are only a few days old.
When a beaver sees danger, it slaps its wide tail
against the water. That makes a loud noise.
The other beavers dive quickly under the water.
They are safe in their lodge.

Beavers talk to each other.
They rub noses, make soft
sounds, and whistle.

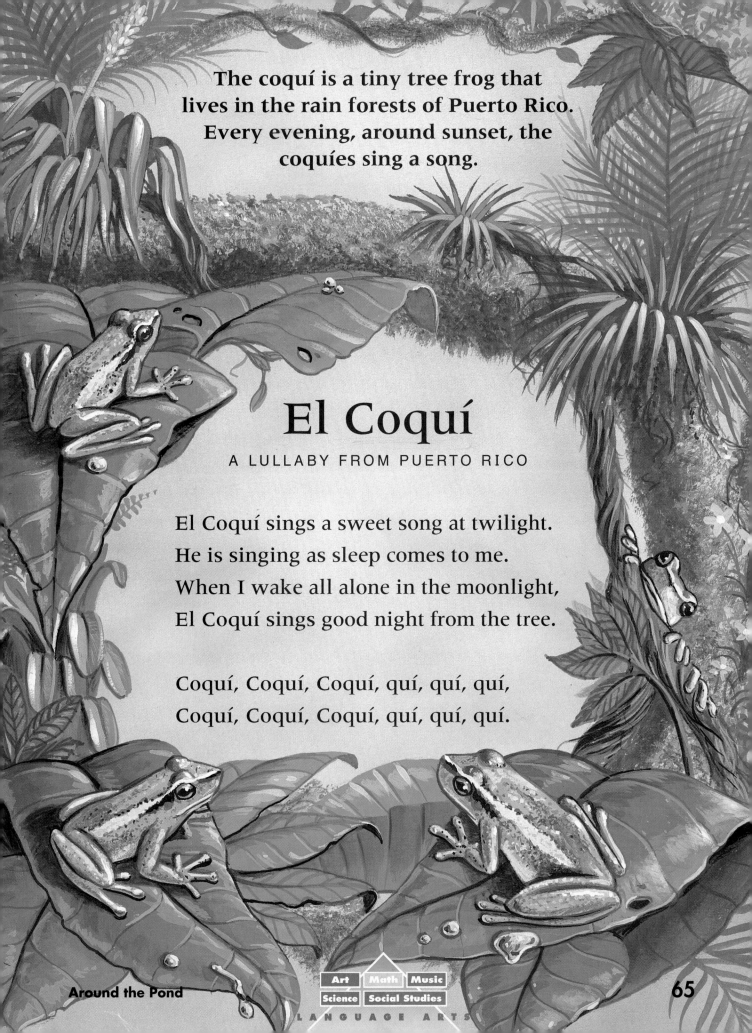

The coquí is a tiny tree frog that lives in the rain forests of Puerto Rico. Every evening, around sunset, the coquíes sing a song.

El Coquí

A LULLABY FROM PUERTO RICO

El Coquí sings a sweet song at twilight.
He is singing as sleep comes to me.
When I wake all alone in the moonlight,
El Coquí sings good night from the tree.

Coquí, Coquí, Coquí, quí, quí, quí,
Coquí, Coquí, Coquí, quí, quí, quí.

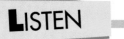 

The Little Lost Coquí

● ● ● ● ● ● ● ● ● ● ● ● ● ● ●

▶ LISTEN

▶ SPEAK

What has happened so far?

▶ THINK

Where do you think Little Rico is?

Self Holistic Portfolio
Traditional Performance
A S S E S S M E N T

READ

"Who is going to look by the pond?" asked Father Coquí.
"I will," shouted Sister Coquí. "Who is going to look under
the palm tree?"
"Brother will," said Father Coquí.

But just then Great-Grandpa Coquí hopped back
to the tree.
Little Rico was on his back!
"Little Rico, Little Rico!" everyone cried.
"I found him behind the mango tree," said Great-Grandpa.
"Little Rico was eating a mosquito for dessert!"

Everyone laughed. Then they all sat around the story tree
and listened to Great-Grandpa's story.

 THINK

What story do you think Great-Grandpa Coquí told?

 WRITE

Have you ever been lost? How did you feel? Write or tell
the story.

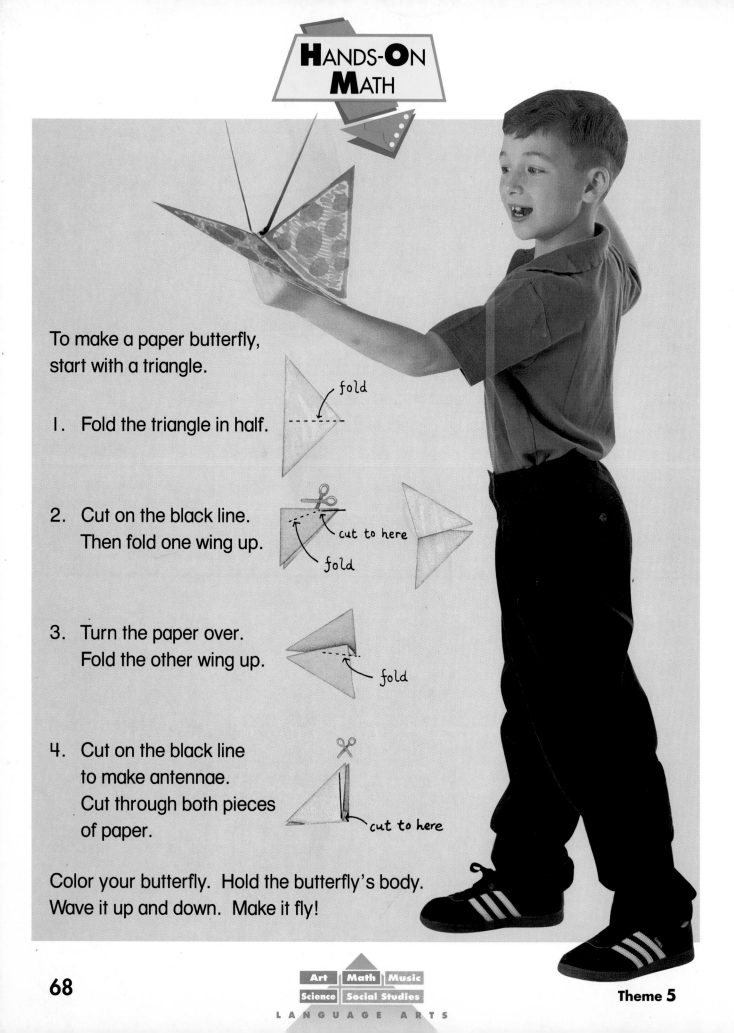

HANDS-ON MATH

To make a paper butterfly, start with a triangle.

1. Fold the triangle in half.

fold

2. Cut on the black line. Then fold one wing up.

cut to here
fold

3. Turn the paper over. Fold the other wing up.

fold

4. Cut on the black line to make antennae. Cut through both pieces of paper.

cut to here

Color your butterfly. Hold the butterfly's body. Wave it up and down. Make it fly!

68

Art | Math | Music
Science | Social Studies

LANGUAGE ARTS

Theme 5

Nature Walk

What kind of bush
does a rabbit sit under
when it rains?

A riddle from Russia

Answer: A wet one!

CLASSES UNDER THE TREES

BY MONICA GUNNING   PICTURES BY FRANÉ LESSAC

My teacher, Miss Zettie, says,
"Children, we can't breathe in here.
Come on! We're going
under the breadfruit tree!"

Art   Math   Music
Science   Social Studies

LANGUAGE ARTS

We leave the one room schoolhouse
these hot days in June
for the breeze outdoors
below blue skies.

Reciting our lessons
in singsong fashion,
we hear twittering birds
recite theirs, too.

The Ungrateful Tiger

A FOLKTALE FROM KOREA

CHARACTERS:

| Storyteller | Tree | Tiger | Ox | Man | Rabbit |

Storyteller A long time ago, a tiger was walking through the jungle. Suddenly, he fell into a deep pit.

Tiger Help, help! Get me out of this pit!

Storyteller Nobody heard the tiger. Nobody came to help. Many days passed. Finally, a man came down the jungle path.

Tiger Please, please help me!

Man I'm sorry, but I can't help you. If I do, you'll eat me up.

Tiger No, no, I won't. I promise I won't. I'll be grateful to you forever.

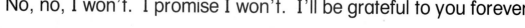

Art Math Music
Science Social Studies

LANGUAGE ARTS

Theme 6

Storyteller The man found a long tree branch, and dropped it into the pit. The tiger climbed up the branch.

Tiger That's better. Say, you look quite delicious, and I'm starving!

Man Wait a minute! You promised you wouldn't eat me.

Tiger Yes, but I didn't realize how hungry I was.

Man That's not fair! I just saved your life. You can't eat me! That would be very ungrateful. Tree, don't you agree with me?

Tree We trees give you shade and fruit to eat. But you cut us down for lumber. Ungrateful—ha! Tiger, enjoy your lunch!

Nature Walk

Man

Wait, wait. Here's an ox.
Ox, don't you agree with me?

Ox

We oxen work hard for you. We carry heavy loads
and plow your land. But when we get old, you kill us
for food. Ungrateful—ha! Tiger, enjoy your lunch.

Man

Wait, wait. Here comes a rabbit. Let's hear what the rabbit says.

Storyteller

The tiger and the man told the rabbit their story. The rabbit listened
very carefully. She stroked her long ears and twitched her nose.

Rabbit

I think I need to see the pit and hear the story again. Lead the way...Now, let me make sure I understand. Tiger, you were up here and the man was in the pit?

Tiger

No, no, that's not right. I was in the pit—like this.

Storyteller

The tiger jumped into the deep pit. The man and the rabbit stared down at the tiger.

Rabbit

The man helped you get out, right?

Tiger

Yes, but...

Rabbit

And in return, you promised not to eat him, right?

Tiger

Yes, but…

Rabbit

And you broke your promise, right?

Tiger

Yes, but…

Rabbit

No "buts" about it, Tiger. You will stay in the pit. The man will go on his way— and so will I.

Storyteller

The tiger roared and roared, deep down in the pit. Then a crow flew by…but that's another story for another time.

76

Put some seeds in a jar with paper.
Add some water.

Wait for the
seeds to sprout.
Mark each day
you wait
on the calendar.

SUN MON TUES WED THURS FRI SAT

SPROUT

How many days
did it take?

Do all seeds take
the same time?

Art Math Music
Science Social Studies
LANGUAGE ARTS

Seasons, Seasons Everywhere!

 LISTEN

 SPEAK

What has happened so far?

 THINK

What season will come next in the United States?
What season will come next in Australia?

Self | Holistic | Portfolio
Traditional | Performance
A S S E S S M E N T

Theme 6

 **READ**

The children said, "It's winter! Let's make a snowman."
They rolled the snow into big balls.
They made a tall snowman. They gave him a hat!

On the same day in Australia, it was summer.
What were the children doing in Australia?
Petting kangaroos at the zoo and sailing on a lake.

 THINK

Could children in the United States see kangaroos
in the summer?

 WRITE

What is your favorite season? What do you like to do
then? Draw and write your answer.

INDEX

TYPES OF LITERATURE
Autobiography 18–20
Biography 48–51
Contemporary fiction 4–7, 8–9, 18–19, 20–23, 24–25
Multicultural folktales 34–38, 56–60, 72–76
Photo essays 21–23, 30–32, 44–46, 62–64
Poetry 33, 55, 61, 70–71
Plays 34–38, 72–76
Riddles/Proverbs 29, 69
Songs and chants 3, 11, 15, 16–17, 39, 43, 47, 65

TOPICS
Alphabet 44–46
Animals 56–60, 61, 62–64, 65
Art 28, 68
Birthday 14
Body parts 8–9
Clothing 8–9
Community spirit 44–46, 48–51
Comparing oneself to others 34–38
Daily routine 47
Days of the week 77
Family 4–7, 15, 16–17, 18–20, 21–23, 24–25
Food 12-13, 18–20, 39, 48–51
Friends 3, 4–7, 8–9, 10, 11, 12–13, 18–19, 30–32, 44–46
Hello in different languages 3
Helping others 12–13, 40–41
Likes/dislikes 4–7, 10
Math 14, 21–23, 42, 52–53, 68, 77
Months of the year 14, 55, 70–71
Music 11, 15, 16–17, 39, 43, 47, 65
Nature 56–60, 62–64, 69, 77
Occupations 44–46
School 3, 4–7, 8–9
Science 42, 54, 61, 62–64, 65, 77
Seasons 55, 70–71
Self-esteem 28, 30–32, 33, 34–38, 44–46
Social studies 3, 4–7, 8–9, 16–17, 18–20, 21–23, 28, 30–32, 44–46, 48–51, 70–71, 78–79
Tangrams 21–23

ACTIVITIES
Alphabetizing 44–46
Conducting
    an interview 28
    a science experiment 42, 54, 77
Creating rhymes and song verses 11, 16–17, 39, 47
Discussing
    points of view 72–76
    predictions 12, 26, 40, 52, 66, 78
Following directions 28, 42, 68
Getting information from photos 21–23, 30–32, 44–46, 62–64
Greeting people 3
Identifying
    body parts 8–9, 39
    clothing 8–9, 39
    objects 8–9, 39
Introducing friends 3, 4–7, 10
Learning about
    beavers 62–64
    coquíes 65
    diverse cultures 3, 8–9, 18–20, 21–23, 28, 29, 44–46, 70–71, 78–79
    Johnny Appleseed 48–51
    lungs and breathing 42
    magnets 54
    planting seeds 77
    real-life children 4–7, 30–32, 44–46
    turtles 61
Listening to/reading a photo essay 21–23, 30–32, 44–46, 62–64
Listening to/reading a play 34–38, 72–76
Listening to/reading a poem 33, 55, 61, 70–71
Listening to/reading a proverb 29
Listening to/reading a riddle 69
Listening to/singing a song/chant 11, 15, 16–17, 43, 47
Listening to/reading a story 4–7, 18–20, 21–23, 24–25
Projects
    counting breaths 42
    experimenting with magnets 54
    making a birthday graph 14
    making a name poster 28
    making a paper butterfly 68
    planting seeds 77
Reading/discussing/dramatizing a folk tale 26–27, 34–38, 56–60, 72–76
Researching the origin of a name 28
Sequencing 34–38
Sharing words in different languages 3, 8–9, 28, 44–46
Summarizing 12, 26, 40, 52, 66, 78
Thinking creatively 12–13, 26–27, 40–41, 52–53, 66–67, 78–79
Writing creatively 13, 27, 28, 41, 53, 67, 79

LINGUISTIC SKILLS
adjectives 10, 55
always/sometimes/never 47
Comparatives and superlatives 34–38
Compound words 65
going to/will 34–38, 48–51
Irregular past tense 16–17, 24–25, 61
Modal: *can* 12–13, 21–23, 29, 33
Plurals 8–9
Simple present tense 4–7, 8–9, 10, 11, 15, 21–23, 30–32, 47, 62–64
Regular past tense 18–20, 44–46, 48–51

HOLISTIC ASSESSMENT
Listening/speaking/reading/writing/thinking skills 12–13, 26–27, 40–41, 52–53, 66–67, 78–79